Michael Vick

Revised Edition

By Jeff Savage

AMAZING ATHLETES

Lerner Publications Company • Minneapolis

Lerner Publications Company
A division of Lerner Publishing Group, Inc.
241 First Avenue North
Minneapolis, MN 55401 U.S.A.

Website address: www.lernerbooks.com

Library of Congress Cataloging-in-Publication Data

Savage, Jeff, 1961–
    Michael Vick / by Jeff Savage. — Rev. ed.
      p.   cm. — (Amazing athletes)
    Includes index.
    ISBN 978–0–7613-8129-7 (pbk. : alk. paper)
    1. Vick, Michael, 1980—Juvenile literature. 2. Football players—United States—Biography—
Juvenile literature. 3. Quarterbacks (Football)—United States—Biography—Juvenile literature.
I. Title.
GV939.V53S38 2012
796.332'092—dc22   2011011448

Manufactured in the United States of America
1 – BP – 7/15/11

TABLE OF CONTENTS

Michael Vick drops back to throw a pass while playing against the Washington Redskins on November 15, 2010.

BACK ON TOP

Philadelphia Eagles' **quarterback** Michael Vick was fired up. On the first play of a game against the Washington Redskins, he looked down the field and launched a pass. The ball sailed deep over the middle to **wide receiver** DeSean Jackson—an 88-yard **touchdown**! Then Michael completed all of his first 10 passes. Michael was on a roll!

Michael chose a perfect time to shine. He was rebuilding his career after several years away from the National Football League (NFL).

The Redskins struggled to put up points. Meanwhile, Michael made play after play. He led a quick drive from the Eagles' 37-yard line with passes to wide receiver Jason Avant and **running back** LeSean McCoy. Then Michael ran it in for a 7-yard touchdown. The Eagles were back in Washington's **red zone** five minutes later. Michael tossed a **shovel pass** to McCoy for another score.

Michael does almost everything with his right hand. But he throws with his left hand.

In the second quarter, with the Redskins **defense** closing in, Michael saw wide receiver Jeremy Maclin moving down the right side of the field. He fired a deep pass. Touchdown!

The Eagles just kept on scoring. By halftime, they were crushing the Redskins, 45–14. Michael threw a 20-yard pass to Avant in the third quarter. He **scrambled** to the right for another 13 yards. Then Michael added one more short touchdown pass.

Michael celebrates after throwing a touchdown pass to Jeremy Maclin against the Redskins.

Michael rushed for 80 yards and two touchdowns during the game against the Redskins.

The Redskins rallied for two touchdowns in the second half. But it wasn't nearly enough. The Eagles won, 59–28.

Michael had passed for 333 yards and four touchdowns. He **rushed** for another 80 yards and two touchdowns. That made him the quarterback with the second most total rushing yards in NFL history. "I've had some great games in my day," Michael said. "But I don't think I've had one quite like this one."

The Eagles moved into first place in their **division** with the win. They knew they had their star quarterback to thank.

Michael's hometown is Newport News, Virginia. Michael's father worked in the city's shipyards.

LEARNING TO THROW

Michael Vick was born June 26, 1980, in Newport News, Virginia. He is the second of four children. His parents are Brenda Vick and Michael Boddie. When Michael was born, his parents were not married and did not live together. Michael's father worked as a painter in the Newport News shipyards.

Brenda Vick raised her children in a three-bedroom apartment in downtown Newport News. To earn extra money for food and clothes, she drove a school bus. When Michael was nine, his parents got married. Michael kept his mother's name of Vick.

Michael grew up loving sports. He enjoyed playing football, baseball, and basketball with his friends.

Even as a youngster, Michael could throw the ball far. Warwick High School coach Tommy Reamon met Michael when he was a ninth grader. "I watched him zip that ball," Reamon remembers, "and I said 'Wow!'"

As a boy, Michael often played with his cousin Aaron Brooks. Aaron *(above)* plays quarterback for the New Orleans Saints.

Coach Reamon saw that Michael had a chance to be a great player. He taught Michael how to get stronger by lifting weights.

He showed him how to build up his arm strength by throwing 100 passes a day.

Coach Reamon also told Michael, "You must learn to read, write, and talk. As a quarterback in America, you must know how to communicate." Michael practiced at home by standing in front of a mirror and talking to himself.

When he wasn't playing football, Michael liked to go fishing. He also liked to play video games with his friends. But Michael loved football best. He was the starting quarterback at Warwick High for three years.

The streets in the town where Michael grew up were not safe. Michael avoided trouble by going fishing. "I would go fishing even if the fish weren't biting," he said. "Just to get out of there."

Michael's amazing speed and arm strength made him a great player. In three seasons, he passed for a whopping 4,846 yards and 43 touchdowns. He was also a great runner and scored 18 rushing touchdowns.

Michael's talents made him a star. Colleges from across the country invited him to play on their football teams. He chose Virginia Tech University in nearby Blacksburg, Virginia.

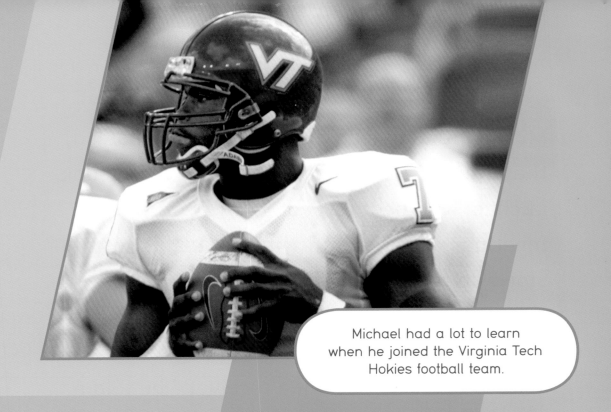

Michael had a lot to learn when he joined the Virginia Tech Hokies football team.

RUNNING OUT FRONT

Playing quarterback is a tough job. A quarterback has to spend many hours studying the team's **playbook**. He has to know what every player on his team is supposed to do on every play. He also has to guess what the other team's defense is going to do on each play.

The Virginia Tech coaches didn't allow Michael to play football his first year. Instead, they wanted him to learn the team's playbook. Michael watched tapes of games and went to meetings. He practiced with the team. But he stood on the sidelines during games.

The team's plays were so difficult that Michael grew frustrated. "I'm going to tell coach I want to play wide receiver," he told a teammate. "This is too much. I can't take it all in." The coaches told him to keep studying and be patient.

After his first year, Michael's hard work started to pay off. Coach Frank Beamer made Michael the **starter** at quarterback. In his first game of the 1999 season, he ran for three touchdowns. He led his team, the Virginia Tech Hokies, to a 47–0 victory.

Michael's amazing play made him big news. Everyone wanted to see this speedy quarterback and his powerful arm. He was one of the most exciting players in college football. As the season continued, Michael led the team to one win after another. The high point of the season came when the Hokies pounded the mighty Syracuse Orangemen 62–0.

The Hokies were unstoppable with Michael as the starting quarterback.

Michael's mom *(center)* is very proud of her son. Coach Beamer *(right)* helped Michael become a great quarterback.

Everyone praised Michael's play. His mother cried at home watching her son's games on TV. "Everything he does is so positive and just so good," she said. "I'm shocked myself, watching him run and throw that ball."

Coach Beamer admired Michael's football skills. But he also admired Michael as a person. "He's kind and polite," said the coach. "He is a good person."

With Michael in charge, the Hokies finished the regular season unbeaten. Their perfect record meant they would compete for the national championship. They faced superpower Florida State in the 2000 **Sugar Bowl**.

Florida State roared to a 28–7 lead. The Hokies were in trouble. Michael gathered his team around him. He said, "Somebody's gotta step up. I guess it's going to be me."

Michael runs for a big gain against the Florida State Seminoles in the 2000 Sugar Bowl.

Michael took over the game. He passed for 225 yards, including a 49-yard touchdown. He ran for 97 yards, including a 3-yard touchdown. He led Virginia Tech to a 29–28 lead. But the powerful Florida State team was just too strong. The Hokies lost the game, 46–29.

Michael sprints down the sideline for another huge gain. Michael played well, but the Hokies couldn't beat the powerful Florida State Seminoles.

NFL commissioner Paul Tagliabue congratulates Michael for being the first player taken in the 2001 NFL Draft.

FLYING HIGH

Michael enjoyed one more great year at Virginia Tech. Then he decided to leave school to join the NFL. The Atlanta Falcons chose Michael as the first pick in the 2001 NFL **Draft**.

Later, Michael signed a six-year **contract** with the Falcons. The Falcons would pay him $62 million. Michael was rich, and he was barely 20 years old!

Falcons coach Dan Reeves wanted Michael to take time to learn the pro game. So once again, Michael spent most of his first year watching and learning. Chris Chandler started the season at quarterback. But Chandler was hurt midway through the season.

Michael *(center)* started his career with the Falcons by watching and learning.

Coach Dan Reeves gave Michael his first chance to play halfway through Michael's first season.

Coach Reeves decided to give Michael a shot. Michael's first game was against the Dallas Cowboys. He threw his first touchdown pass and also ran for 40 yards. Best of all, he led the Falcons to a 20–13 win.

After the season ended, the Falcons let Chandler leave the team. Michael would be the team's new starter at quarterback for 2002.

Michael had a terrific season his second year.

Michael took the NFL by storm in 2002. No one had ever seen such a mixture of speed and arm strength. When Michael scrambled with the ball, players struggled to catch and tackle him. And Michael's powerful passes shot right past them.

Michael's skills helped lead the Falcons to nine wins and a spot in the **playoffs**. His great play also won him a place in the **Pro Bowl**.

The Falcons faced the Green Bay Packers in the playoffs. Michael started the game hot. He helped the Falcons earn a quick 7–0 lead with a great pass to wide receiver Shawn Jefferson. Later in the first quarter, the Falcons struck for another score and a 14–0 lead. The Falcons won the game easily, 27–7.

Michael runs past Green Bay Packers players for a big gain. The Packers couldn't stop Michael throughout the game.

Packers quarterback Brett Favre told Michael, "You're going to be a superstar in this league."

The Falcons' playoff run ended the next week with a loss to the Philadelphia Eagles. Then, in 2003, Michael broke his leg in a **preseason** game. He was out for most of the season. The Falcons won just five games, and Coach Reeves was fired. But the Falcons did not improve much during several seasons under coach Jim Mora.

Packers star quarterback Brett Favre *(right)* congratulates Michael after his great performance in their 2003 playoff game.

Michael prepares to talk to the media about his involvement in an illegal dogfighting ring.

SECOND CHANCE

In 2007, Michael got into trouble with the law. Police discovered that he had been running an illegal dogfighting ring in Virginia. Dogfighting pits animals against one another. Often two dogs fight until one of them is dead. People bet on the fights.

The NFL suspended Michael. In November 2007, he went to jail for almost two years.

"I got a lot to think about," he said. "I offer my deepest apologies to everybody." He was especially sorry to let down his young fans.

In 2009, Michael was a free man. The NFL allowed him to join a team again. He joined the Philadelphia Eagles as a backup for quarterback Donovan McNabb.

The Eagles played Atlanta in December 2009.

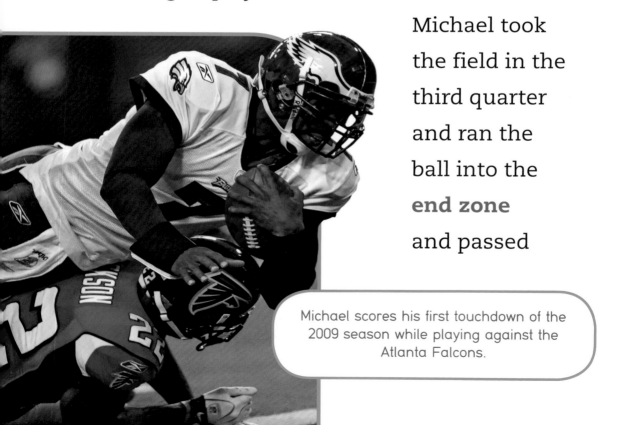

Michael took the field in the third quarter and ran the ball into the **end zone** and passed

Michael scores his first touchdown of the 2009 season while playing against the Atlanta Falcons.

for another six points. With a 34–7 Eagles victory, Vick showed he could still perform like a star.

Kevin Kolb became quarterback for the Eagles in 2010. But he was injured in week 1. Suddenly Michael was a starter again! He passed for nearly 300 yards in wins against Detroit and Jacksonville. Then he wowed fans with his record-setting stats against the Redskins. The Eagles won their way to a spot in the playoffs.

Once again, they faced the Packers. Green Bay scored a 14–3 lead with quarterback Aaron Rodgers. Then Michael took charge. He got them to within one score.

The Eagles were excited to add Michael to their team. Head coach Andy Reid said, "He's an unbelievable athlete, both running the ball and throwing it."

Trailing 21–16, the Eagles got one more shot. Michael threw deep. But the pass was intercepted. The season was over.

"It's not the way I wanted to go out," Michael said. "I have to learn from it." The 2010 season had been Michael's best yet. The Eagles signed him to another one-year contract in 2011.

The Eagles know their star will keep working to be the best. If he prepares well, Michael says, "Then, there's no stopping me."

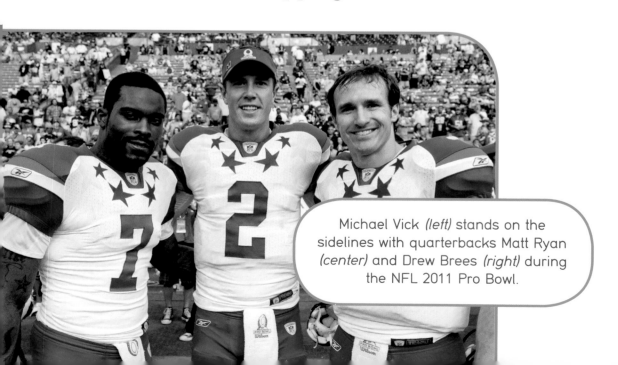

Michael Vick (left) stands on the sidelines with quarterbacks Matt Ryan (center) and Drew Brees (right) during the NFL 2011 Pro Bowl.

Selected Career Highlights

2010 Passed for 3,018 yards and 21 touchdowns, rushed for another nine
Led the Eagles to the National Football Conference (NFC) Wild Card
   playoff game
Selected to the Pro Bowl for the fourth time
Became the first NFL player with at least 300 yards passing,
   50 yards rushing, four passing touchdowns, and two rushing
   touchdowns in one game

2009 Returned to the NFL as a quarterback for the Philadelphia Eagles
Received the Ed Block Courage Award for the Eagles (voted on by
   his teammates)

2007 Suspended from the NFL for running a dogfighting ring

2006 Led all NFL quarterbacks with 1,039 yards rushing

2004 Led all NFL quarterbacks with 902 yards rushing
Led the Atlanta Falcons to an 11–5 record
Led the Falcons to a 47–17 playoff win over the St. Louis Rams

2003 Rushed for 141 yards in one game, the third-highest total for a
   quarterback in NFL history

2002 Ran for 1,066 yards in his first two pro seasons, more than any
   other quarterback
Led the Falcons to a 27–7 playoff victory
   against the Green Bay Packers
Selected to the Pro Bowl for the first time

2001 First player selected overall in the
   NFL draft

2000 Passed for 1,234 yards and rushed for
   607 yards
Finished his Virginia Tech career
   with a 20–1 regular season record
   as a starter

1999 Led Virginia Tech to a perfect 11–0
   regular season
Won the Archie Griffin Award as
   college football Player of the Year

Glossary

contract: a written deal signed by a player and his or her team. The player agrees to play for the team for a certain number of years. The team agrees to pay the player a certain amount of money.

defense: the team of 11 players that doesn't have the football. The defense tries to stop the other team from scoring.

division: a group of four teams in the NFL. The team with the best record in each division at the end of the season goes to the playoffs.

draft: a yearly event in which teams choose new players from a selected group

end zone: the area beyond the goal line at each end of the field. A team scores a touchdown when it reaches the other team's end zone.

playbook: a collection of plays a team will use in games

playoffs: a series of games held every year to decide a league champion

preseason: practice games played before the regular season begins

Pro Bowl: a game held every year after the season in which the best NFL players compete

quarterback: the football player whose job it is to pass the ball and call the plays. The quarterback is the leader of the offense.

red zone: the area between the 20-yard line and the end zone of the defensive team

running back: a player whose job it is to run with the ball

rushed: ran with the football

scrambled: ran around with the ball before throwing it

shovel pass: a short pass thrown with an underhand or backhand toss

starter: a person who is named to play from the beginning of the game

Sugar Bowl: a college football game played every year in the Super Dome in New Orleans, Louisiana

touchdown: a six-point score. A team scores a touchdown when it gets into the other team's end zone with the ball.

wide receiver: a player who catches passes

Further Reading & Websites

Goodman, Michael, E. *The History of the Atlanta Falcons*. Mankato, MN: Creative Education, 2005.

Jacobs, Greg. *The Everything Kids' Football Book*. Avon, MA: Adams Media, 2010.

Kennedy, Mike, and Mark Stewart. *Touchdown: The Power and Precision of Football's Perfect Play*. Minneapolis: Millbrook Press, 2010.

Savage, Jeff. *Aaron Rodgers*. Minneapolis: Lerner Publications Company, 2012.

The Official Site of the National Football League
http://nfl.com
The NFL's official website has news, scores, photos, video highlights, and information on all teams and players, including Michael Vick and the Philadelphia Eagles.

Sports Illustrated Kids
http://www.sikids.com
The *Sports Illustrated Kids* website covers all sports, including NFL football.

Index

Photo Acknowledgments

The images in this book are used with the permission of: AP Photo/Paul Spinelli, p. 4; AP Photo/Gail Burton, p. 6; AP Photo/Nick Wass, p. 7; © Tim Wright/CORBIS, p. 8; © David Allio/Icon SMI/ZUMA Press, p. 10; © Gary I. Rothstein/Icon SMI, p. 13; © Doug Pensinger/Getty Images, p. 15; © Wayne Scarberry/AFP/Getty Images, p. 16; © Matthew Stockman/Getty Images, p. 17; © Brian Bahr/Getty Images, p. 18; © Mike Segar/Reuters/CORBIS, p. 19; © SportsChrome East/West, Rob Tringali, pp. 20, 21, 22; © Jonathan Stringer/Getty Images, p. 23; © David Stluka, p. 24; AP Photo/Richmond Times-Dispatch, Bob Brown, p. 25; © Drew Hallowell/Getty Images, p. 26; AP Photo/Jim Mahoney, p. 28; © Al Bello/Getty Images, p. 29.

Front Cover: © Rob Tringali/SportsChrome/Getty Images.

Main body text set in Caecilia LT std 55 Roman 16/28. Typeface provided by Linotype AG.